D1149981

CODE ON
NOISE LEVELS
ON BOARD SHIPS

2014 EDITION

IMO INTERNATIONAL MARITIME ORGANIZATION

London, 2014

First published in 2014
by the INTERNATIONAL MARITIME ORGANIZATION
4 Albert Embankment, London SE1 7SR
www.imo.org

Printed by Polestar Wheatons (UK) Ltd, Exeter, EX2 8RP

ISBN 978-92-801-1578-9

IMO PUBLICATION
Sales number: I817E

This publication has been prepared from official documents of IMO, and every effort
has been made to eliminate errors and reproduce the original text(s) faithfully. Readers
should be aware that, in case of inconsistency, the official IMO text will prevail.

075406

Contents

Foreword

1   The Code on noise levels on board ships (hereinafter referred to as "the Code") has been developed to provide international standards for protection against noise regulated by regulation II-1/3-12 of the International Convention for the Safety of Life at Sea (SOLAS), 1974, as amended. Although the Code is legally treated as a mandatory instrument under the SOLAS Convention, certain provisions of the Code remain recommendatory or informative (see paragraph 1.1.3).

2   These regulations, recommendations and advice are intended to provide Administrations with the tools to promote "hearing saving" environments on board ships. This is, however, a dynamic topic, dealing with the human and technical environments in which they interface. Rules and recommendations will necessarily evolve, on a case-by-case basis, as a result of various technological as well as safety management practice developments. For this reason Administrations are encouraged to pass on experience and information received from recognized organizations, ship operators and equipment designers to improve this Code.

3   The Code has been developed having regard to conventional passenger and cargo ships. While certain types and sizes of ships have been excluded from its application, it should be recognized that full application to ships which differ appreciably from the conventional types of ships regarding design or operations might need specific consideration.

4   The Organization adopted a Recommendation on methods of measuring noise levels at listening posts (resolution A.343(IX)), which this Code is not intended to supersede. That Recommendation relates to interference by shipborne noise with the proper reception of external audible navigation signals and although the methods of measuring noise levels in accordance with the Recommendation and with the Code differ, these documents are to be considered compatible inasmuch as this Code is concerned primarily with the effect of noise on health and comfort. Care will be needed to ensure that there is compatibility between the general requirements and the requirements for audibility of navigation signals.

Resolution MSC.337(91)
(adopted on 30 November 2012)

Code on noise levels on board ships

THE MARITIME SAFETY COMMITTEE,

RECALLING Article 28(b) of the Convention on the International Maritime Organization concerning the functions of the Committee,

RECALLING ALSO resolutions A.343(IX) and A.468(XII) by which the Assembly of the Organization adopted the Recommendation on methods of measuring noise levels at listening posts and the Code on noise levels on board ships, respectively,

RECOGNIZING the need to establish mandatory noise level limits for machinery spaces, control rooms, workshops, accommodation and other spaces on board ships, taking into account experience gained with regard to noise control and allowable exposure levels since the adoption of resolution A.468(XII),

NOTING regulation II-1/3-12 of the International Convention for the Safety of Life at Sea (SOLAS), 1974, as amended (hereinafter referred to as "the Convention"), adopted by resolution MSC.338(91), concerning protection against noise,

NOTING ALSO that the aforementioned regulation II-1/3-12 provides that ships shall be constructed to reduce on-board noise and to protect personnel from noise in accordance with the Code on noise levels on board ships (hereinafter referred to as "the Code"),

HAVING CONSIDERED, at its ninety-first session, the recommendation made by the Sub-Committee on Ship Design and Equipment, at its fifty-sixth session,

1   ADOPTS the Code on noise levels on board ships, the text of which is set out in the annex to the present resolution;

2   INVITES Contracting Governments to the Convention to note that the Code will take effect on 1 July 2014 upon entry into force of regulation II-1/3-12 of the Convention;

3   REQUESTS the Secretary-General to transmit certified copies of this resolution and the text of the Code, contained in the annex, to all Contracting Governments to the Convention;

4   ALSO REQUESTS the Secretary-General to transmit copies of this resolution and the annex to all Members of the Organization which are not Contracting Governments to the Convention.

Chapter 1
General

1.1   Scope

1.1.1   The Code is intended to provide standards to prevent the occurrence of potentially hazardous noise levels on board ships and to provide standards for an acceptable environment for seafarers. These standards were developed to address passenger and cargo ships. Since some sizes and certain service types of ships have been exempted from these requirements, it should be recognized that full application of the Code to ships that differ appreciably from conventional ships will require special considerations. The Code is intended to provide the basis for a design standard, with compliance based on the satisfactory conclusion of sea trials that result in issuance of a Noise Survey Report. Ongoing operational compliance is predicated on the crew being trained in the principles of personal protection and maintenance of mitigation measures. These would be enforced under the dynamic processes and practices put in place under SOLAS chapter IX.

1.1.2   Requirements and recommendations are made for:

.1   measurement of noise levels and exposure;

.2   protecting the seafarer from the risk of noise-induced hearing loss under conditions where at present it is not feasible to limit the noise to a level which is not potentially harmful;

.3   limits on acceptable maximum noise levels for all spaces to which seafarers normally have access; and

.4   verification of acoustic insulation between accommodation spaces.

1.1.3   Although this Code is legally treated as a mandatory instrument under the SOLAS Convention, the following provisions of this Code remain recommendatory, options for compliance, or informative in nature:

–   paragraphs 1.3.2 and 1.3.3

- paragraphs 3.4.2 and 3.4.3
- chapter 5
- section 6.3
- section 7.3
- appendix 2
- appendix 3
- appendix 4

1.2   Purpose

The purpose of the Code is to limit noise levels and to reduce seafarers' exposure to noise, in order to:

.1   provide for safe working conditions by giving consideration to the need for speech communication and for hearing audible alarms, and to an environment where clear-headed decisions can be made in control stations, navigation and radio spaces and manned machinery spaces;

.2   protect the seafarer from excessive noise levels which may give rise to a noise-induced hearing loss; and

.3   provide the seafarer with an acceptable degree of comfort in rest, recreation and other spaces and also provide conditions for recuperation from the effects of exposure to high noise levels.

1.3   Application

1.3.1   The Code applies to new ships of a gross tonnage of 1,600 and above.

1.3.2   The specific provisions relating to potentially hazardous noise levels, mitigation and personal protective gear contained in the Code may be applied to existing ships of a gross tonnage of 1,600 and above, as far as reasonable and practical, to the satisfaction of the Administration.

1.3.3   The Code may be applied to new ships of a gross tonnage of less than 1,600 as far as reasonable and practical, to the satisfaction of the Administration.

1.3.4   The Code does not apply to:

    .1   dynamically supported craft;

    .2   high-speed craft;

    .3   fishing vessels;

    .4   pipe-laying barges;

    .5   crane barges;

    .6   mobile offshore drilling units;

    .7   pleasure yachts not engaged in trade;

    .8   ships of war and troopships;

    .9   ships not propelled by mechanical means;

    .10   pile driving vessels; and

    .11   dredgers.

1.3.5   The Code applies to ships in port or at sea with seafarers on board.

1.3.6   Dispensations from certain requirements may in special circumstances be granted by the Administration, if it is documented that compliance will not be possible despite relevant and reasonable technical noise reduction measures. Such dispensation shall not include cabins, unless exceptional circumstances prevail. If dispensation is granted, it shall be ensured that the goal of this Code is achieved, and the noise exposure limits shall be considered in conjunction with chapter 5.

1.3.7   For ships designed for and employed on voyages of short duration, or on other services involving short periods of operation of the ship, to the satisfaction of the Administration, paragraphs 4.2.3 and 4.2.4 may be applied only with the ship in the port condition, provided that the periods under such conditions are adequate for seafarers' rest and recreation.

1.3.8   The Code is not intended to apply to passenger cabins and other passenger spaces, except in so far as they are work spaces and are covered by the provisions of the Code.

1.3.9   In case of repairs, alterations and modifications of a major character and outfitting related thereto of existing ships, it shall be ensured that areas, in which changes have been made, meet the requirements of this Code for new ships, insofar as the Administration deems reasonable and practicable.

1.3.10   The Code covers only noise sources related to the ship such as machinery and propulsion but does not include wind/wave/ice noise, alarms, public address systems, etc.

1.4   Definitions

For the purpose of the Code the following definitions apply. Additional definitions are given elsewhere in the Code.

1.4.1   *Accommodation spaces* are cabins, offices (for carrying out a ship's business), hospitals, meal rooms, recreation rooms (such as lounges, smoking rooms, cinemas, gymnasiums, libraries, and hobbies and games rooms) and open recreation areas to be used by seafarers.

1.4.2   *Apparent weighted sound reduction index* (R'_w) means a single number value expressed in decibels (dB) which describes the overall sound insulation performance of in situ walls, doors or floors (see ISO 717-1:1996, as amended by 1:2013).

1.4.3   *A-weighted equivalent continuous sound level* ($L_{Aeq,T}$) means the A-weighted sound pressure level of a continuous steady sound that, within a measurement time interval, T, has the same mean square sound pressure as a sound under consideration which varies with time. It is expressed in decibels A (dB(A)) and is given by the following equation:

$$L_{Aeq,T} = 10\log \frac{1}{T} \int_0^T \frac{p_A(t)^2}{p_0^2} \cdot dt$$

where:

T = measurement time

$p_A(t)$ = A-weighted instantaneous sound pressure

p_0 = 20 μPa (the reference level)

1.4.4   *A-weighted sound pressure level or noise level* means the quantity measured by a sound level meter in which the frequency response is weighted according to the A-weighting curve (see IEC 61672-1 (2002)).

1.4.5 *C-weighted equivalent continuous sound level* ($L_{Ceq,T}$) means the C-weighted sound pressure level of a continuous steady sound that within a measurement time interval, T, has the same mean square sound pressure as a sound under consideration which varies with time. It is expressed in decibels C (dB(C)) and is given by the following equation:

$$L_{Ceq,T} = 10\log \frac{1}{T} \int_0^T \frac{p_C(t)^2}{p_0^2} \cdot dt$$

where:

T = measurement time

$p_C(t)$ = C-weighted instantaneous sound pressure

p_0 = 20 µPa (the reference level)

1.4.6 *C-weighted peak sound level* (L_{Cpeak}) means the C-weighted maximum instantaneous sound pressure level. It is expressed in decibels C (dB(C)) and is given by the following equation:

$$L_{Cpeak} = 10\log \frac{p_{peak}^2}{p_0^2}$$

where:

p_{peak} = C-weighted maximum instantaneous sound pressure

p_0 = 20 µPa (the reference level)

1.4.7 *C-weighted sound pressure level or noise level* means the quantity measured by a sound level meter in which the frequency response is weighted according to the C-weighting curve (see IEC 61672-1 (2002)).

1.4.8 *Continuously manned spaces* are spaces in which the continuous or prolonged presence of seafarers is necessary for normal operational periods.

1.4.9 *Crane barge* means a vessel with permanently installed cranes designed principally for lifting operations.

1.4.10 *Daily noise exposure level* ($L_{ex,24h}$) represents the equivalent noise exposure level for a period of 24 h and is given by the following equation:

$$L_{ex,24h} = L_{Aeq,T} + 10\log(\frac{T}{T_0})$$

where:

T is the effective duration on board

T_0 is the reference duration 24 h

The total equivalent continuous A-weighted sound pressure level $(L_{Aeq,T})$ shall be calculated by using the different noise levels (L_{Aeq,T_i}) and associated time periods with the following equation:

$$L_{Aeq,T} = 10\log \frac{1}{T} \sum_{i=1}^{n} (T_i \times 10^{0,1 L_{Aeq,T_i}})$$

where:

$L_{Aeq,Ti}$ is the equivalent continuous A-weighted sound pressure level, in decibels, averaged over time interval T_i:

$$T = \sum_{i=1}^{n} T_i$$

$L_{ex,24h} = L_{Aeq,24h}$ when seafarers are on board over a period of 24 h.

1.4.11 *Dredger* means a vessel undertaking operations to excavate bottom sediment, where the vessel has permanently installed excavation equipment.

1.4.12 *Duty stations* are those spaces in which the main navigating equipment, the ship's radio or the emergency source of power are located or where the fire recording or fire control equipment is centralized and also those spaces used for galleys, main pantries, stores (except isolated pantries and lockers), mail and specie rooms, workshops other than those forming part of the machinery spaces and similar such spaces.

1.4.13 *Dynamically-supported craft* means a craft which is operable on or above water and which has characteristics different from those of conventional displacement ships. Within the aforementioned generality, a craft which complies with either of the following characteristics:

.1 the weight, or a significant part thereof, is balanced in one mode of operation by other than hydrostatic forces;

.2 the craft is able to operate at speeds such that the function $\frac{v}{\sqrt{gL}}$ is equal to or greater than 0.9, where v is the maximum speed, L is the water-line length and g is the acceleration due to gravity, all in consistent units.

1.4.14 *Existing ship* means a ship which is not a new ship.

1.4.15 *Fishing vessel* means a vessel used commercially for catching fish, whales, seals, walrus or other living resources of the sea.

1.4.16   *Hearing loss* is evaluated in relation to a reference auditory threshold defined conventionally in ISO Standard 389-1 (1998). The hearing loss corresponds to the difference between the auditory threshold of the subject being examined and the reference auditory threshold.

1.4.17   *Hearing protector* means a device worn to reduce the level of noise reaching the ears. Passive noise-cancelling headsets block noise from reaching the ear. Active noise-cancelling headphones generate a signal that cancels out the ambient noise within the headphone.

1.4.18   *Integrating sound level meter* means a sound level meter designed or adapted to measure the level of the mean squared time averaged A-weighted and C-weighted sound pressure.

1.4.19   *Machinery spaces* are any space which contains steam or internal-combustion machinery, pumps, air compressors, boilers, oil fuel units, major electrical machinery, oil filling stations, thrusters, refrigerating, stabilizing, steering gear, ventilation and air conditioning machinery, etc. and trunks to such spaces.

1.4.20   *Mobile offshore drilling unit* means a vessel capable of engaging in drilling operations for the exploration for, or exploitation of, resources beneath the seabed, such as liquid or gaseous hydrocarbons, sulphur or salt.

1.4.21   *Navigating bridge wings* are those parts of the ship's navigating bridge extending towards the ship's sides.

1.4.22   *New ship* means a ship to which this Code applies in accordance with SOLAS regulation II-1/3-12.1.

1.4.23   *Noise*, for the purpose of the Code, is all sound which can result in hearing impairment, or which can be harmful to health or be otherwise dangerous or disruptive.

1.4.24   *Noise-induced hearing loss* is hearing loss, originating in the nerve cells within the cochlea, attributable to the effects of sound.

1.4.25   *Noise level* is defined in paragraph 1.4.4 describing A-weighted sound pressure level.

1.4.26   *Occasional exposures* are those exposures typically occurring once per week, or less frequently.

1.4.27   *Pile-driving vessel* means a vessel undertaking operations to install pilings in the seabed.

1.4.28 *Pipe-laying barge* means a vessel specifically constructed for, or used in conjunction with, operations associated with the laying of submarine pipelines.

1.4.29 *Port condition* means the condition in which all machinery solely required for propulsion is stopped.

1.4.30 *Potentially hazardous noise levels* are those levels at and above which persons exposed to them without protection are at risk of sustaining a noise-induced hearing loss.

1.4.31 *Repairs, alterations and modifications of a major character* means a conversion of a ship which substantially alters the dimensions, carrying capacity or engine power of the ship, which changes the type of the ship, or which otherwise so alters the ship that, if it were a new ship, it would become subject to the relevant provisions.

1.4.32 *Sound* is energy that is transmitted by pressure waves in air or other materials and is the objective cause of the sensation of hearing.

1.4.33 *Sound pressure level* (L_p or SPL) means sound pressure level expressed, in decibel (dB), of a sound or noise given by the following equation:

$$L_p = 10 \log \frac{p^2}{p_0{}^2}$$

where:

p = sound pressure, in pascal (Pa)

p_0 = 20 µPa (the reference level)

1.4.34 *Voyages of short duration* are voyages where the ship is not generally underway for periods long enough for seafarers to require sleep, or long off-duty periods, during the voyages.

1.4.35 *Weighted sound reduction index* (R_w) means a single number value, expressed in decibels (dB), which describes the overall sound insulation performance (in the laboratory) of walls, doors or floors (see ISO 717-1:1997, as amended by 1:2013).

Chapter 2
Measuring equipment

2.1 Equipment specifications

2.1.1 Sound level meters

Measurement of sound pressure levels shall be carried out using precision integrating sound level meters subject to the requirements of this chapter. Such meters shall be manufactured to IEC 61672-1 (2002)[*] type/class 1 standard as applicable, or to an equivalent standard acceptable to the Administration.[†]

2.1.2 Octave filter set

When used alone, or in conjunction with a sound level meter, as appropriate, an octave filter set shall conform to IEC 61260 (1995)[‡] or an equivalent standard acceptable to the Administration.

2.2 Use of equipment

2.2.1 Calibration

Sound calibrators shall comply with the standard IEC 60942 (2003) and shall be approved by the manufacturer of the sound level meter used.

2.2.2 Check of measuring instrument and calibrator

Calibrator and sound level meter shall be verified at least every two years by a national standard laboratory or a competent laboratory accredited according to ISO 17025 (2005) as corrected by (Cor 1:2006).

---

[*] Recommendation for sound level meters.

[†] Sound level meters class or type 1, manufactured according to IEC 651/IEC 804, may be used until 1 July 2016.

[‡] Octave-band and fractional-octave-band filters.

2.2.3 *Microphone wind screen*

A microphone wind screen shall be used when taking readings outside, e.g. on navigating bridge wings or on deck, and below deck where there is any substantial air movement. The wind screen should not affect the measurement level of similar sounds by more than 0.5 dB(A) in "no wind" conditions.

Chapter 3
Measurement

3.1 General

3.1.1   On completion of the construction of the ship, or as soon as practicable thereafter, measurement of noise levels in all spaces specified in chapter 4 shall take place under the operating conditions specified in sections 3.3 and 3.4 and shall be suitably recorded as required by section 4.3.

3.1.2   Measurements of the A-weighted equivalent continuous sound level ($L_{Aeq,T}$) shall be made for the purpose of ensuring compliance with chapter 4.

3.1.3   Measurements of the C-weighted equivalent continuous sound level ($L_{Ceq,T}$) and the C-weighted peak sound level (L_{Cpeak}) shall be made in spaces where $L_{Aeq,T}$ exceeds 85 dB(A) for the purpose of determining appropriate hearing protection according to the HML-method (see chapter 7 and appendix 2).

3.2 Personnel requirements

3.2.1   In order to ensure an acceptable and comparable quality of the measurement results and the reports the measuring institutes or experts shall prove their competence with view to noise measurements.

3.2.2   This person conducting measurements shall have:[*]

    .1   knowledge in the field of noise, sound measurements and handling of used equipment;

    .2   training concerning the procedures specified in this Code.

---

[*] Testing institutions which support a quality management system according to ISO 17020/25 are considered to fulfil these requirements.

3.3   Operating conditions at sea trials

3.3.1   Measurements should be taken with the ship in the loaded or ballast condition. The course of the ship shall be as straight as possible. The actual conditions during the measurements shall be recorded on the survey report.

3.3.2   Noise measurements shall be taken at normal service speed and, unless otherwise addressed in the provisions below, no less than 80% of the maximum continuous rating (MCR). Controllable pitch and Voith-Schneider propellers, if any, shall be in the normal seagoing position. For special ship types and for ships with special propulsion and power configurations, such as diesel-electric systems, the Administration may, in cooperation with the shipyard and shipowners, give due consideration to actual ship design or operating parameters when applying the requirements of paragraphs 3.3.1 and 3.3.2.

3.3.3   All machinery, navigation instruments, radio and radar sets, etc. normally in use at normal seagoing condition and levels, including squelch shall operate throughout the measurement period. However, neither energized fog signals nor helicopter operations shall take place during the taking of these measurements.

3.3.4   Measurements in spaces containing emergency diesel engine driven generators, fire pumps or other emergency equipment that would normally be run only in emergency, or for test purposes, shall be taken with the equipment operating. Measurements are not intended for determining compliance with maximum noise level limits, but as a reference for personal protection of seafarers carrying out maintenance, repair and test activities in such spaces.

3.3.5   Mechanical ventilation, heating and air-conditioning equipment shall be in normal operation, taking into account that the capacity shall be in accordance with the design conditions.

3.3.6   Doors and windows should in general be closed.

3.3.7   Spaces should be furnished with all necessary equipment. Measurements without soft furnishings may be taken but no allowance should be made for their absence. Rechecks or follow-up readings may be taken with soft furnishings included.

3.3.8   Ships fitted with bow thrusters, stabilizers, etc. may be subject to high noise levels when this machinery is in operation. For thrusters, measurements shall be made at 40% thruster power and the ship's speed shall be appropriate for thruster operation. Measurements shall be taken at positions around such machinery when in operation and in adjacent accommodation spaces and duty stations. If such equipment is intended for continuous operation, e.g. stabilizers, measurements shall be made for ensuring compliance with chapter 4. If such systems are intended for short temporary use only, for instance during port manoeuvres, measurements are only relevant for ensuring compliance with chapter 5 on noise exposure.

3.3.9   In case of ships with dynamical positioning (DP), which is intended for use in normal working condition, additional noise measurements at DP mode shall be made at control stations, duty stations, and accommodation spaces to ensure that the maximum noise level limits in these spaces are not exceeded. The Administration, classification societies, shipyard and DP designers, as appropriate, shall agree on a process to simulate the operation of the DP thruster system under conditions which would approximate station-holding at or above 40% of maximum thruster power for design environmental conditions that the ship operates in.

3.4   Operating conditions in port

3.4.1   Measurements as specified in paragraphs 3.4.2, 3.4.3 and 3.4.4 relate to the ship in port condition.

3.4.2   When the noise from the ship's cargo handling equipment may lead to noise above maximum levels in duty stations and accommodation spaces affected by its operation, measurements should be taken. Noise originating from sources external to the ship should be discounted as indicated in paragraph 3.5.3.

3.4.3   Where the ship is a vehicle carrier and noise during loading and discharging originates from vehicles, the noise level in the cargo spaces and the duration of the exposure should be considered in conjunction with chapter 5. Such noise levels originating from vehicles may be estimated theoretically by the shipyard and shipowners in cooperation with the Administration.

3.4.4   Measurements shall be taken in machinery spaces with the machinery operating in the port condition if the provisions of paragraph 5.3.5 in respect of hearing protection shall be met in lieu of the provisions of paragraph 4.2.1 during maintenance, overhaul or similar port conditions.

3.5   Environmental conditions

3.5.1   The readings obtained may be affected if the water depth is less than five times the draught or if there are large reflecting surfaces in the ship's vicinity. Such conditions shall therefore be noted in the noise survey report.

3.5.2 The meteorological conditions such as wind and rain, as well as sea state, should be such that they do not influence the measurements. Wind force 4 and 1 m wave height should not be exceeded. If this cannot be achieved, the actual conditions shall be reported.

3.5.3 Care shall be taken to see that noise from extraneous sound sources, such as people, entertainment, construction and repair work, does not influence the noise level on board the ship at the positions of measurement. If necessary, measured values may be corrected for steady state background noise according to the energy summation principle.

3.6 Measurement procedures

3.6.1 During noise level measurement, only seafarers necessary for the operation of the ship and persons taking the measurements shall be present in the space concerned.

3.6.2 Sound pressure level readings shall be taken in decibels using an A-weighting (dB(A)) and C-weighting (dB(C)) filter and if necessary also in octave bands between 31.5 and 8,000 Hz.

3.6.3 The noise level measurements shall be taken with the integrating sound level meter using spatial averaging (as described in paragraph 3.13.1) and over a time period until stable readings are found or at least 15 s in order to represent the average value from variations due to irregular operation or variations in the sound field. Readings shall be made only to the nearest decibel. If first decimal of the dB reading is 5 or higher, the reading shall be made to nearest higher integer.

3.7 Determination of noise exposure

In addition to the continuous sound level measurements the noise exposure level of seafarers (see chapter 5) shall be determined based upon ISO 9612:2009. A simplified procedure based on ISO 9612 and a workplace-related noise exposure is given in appendix 4.

3.8 Calibration

The sound level meter shall be calibrated with the calibrator referred to in paragraph 2.2.1 before and after measurements are taken.

3.9   Measurement uncertainties

The uncertainty of measurements on board vessels depends on several factors, for example, measurement techniques and environmental conditions. Measurements made in conformity with this Code with few exceptions result in reproducibility standard deviation of the equivalent continuous A-weighted sound pressure level equal to or less than 1.5 dB.

3.10   Points of measurement

3.10.1   *Measurement positions*

If not otherwise stated, measurements shall be taken with the microphone at a height of between 1.2 m (seated person) and 1.6 m (standing person) from the deck. The distance between two measurement points should be at least 2 m, and in large spaces not containing machinery, measurements should be taken at intervals not greater than 10 m throughout the space including positions of maximum noise level. In no case shall measurements be taken closer than 0.5 m from the boundaries of a space. The microphone positions shall be as specified in paragraphs 3.10.3 and sections 3.11 to 3.14. Measurements shall be taken at positions where the personnel work, including at communication stations.

3.10.2   *Duty stations*

The noise level shall be measured at all points where the work is carried out. Additional measurements shall be performed in spaces containing duty stations if variations in noise level are thought to occur in the vicinity of the duty stations.

3.10.3   *Intake and exhaust openings*

When measuring noise levels, the microphone should, where possible, not be placed within a 30° angle away from the direction of the gas stream and not less than a distance of 1 m from the edge of the intake or exhaust opening of engines, ventilation, air conditioning and cooler systems, and as far as possible from reflecting surfaces.

3.11   Measurements in machinery spaces

3.11.1   Measurements shall be taken at the principal working and control stations of the seafarers in the machinery spaces and in the adjacent control rooms, if any, special attention being paid to telephone locations and to positions where voice communication and audible signals are important.

3.11.2 Measurements should not normally be taken closer than 1 m from operating machinery, or from decks, bulkheads or other large surfaces, or from air inlets. Where this is not possible, measurement shall be taken at a position midway between the machinery and adjacent reflecting surface.

3.11.3 Measurements from machinery which constitutes a sound source should be taken at 1 m from the machinery. Measurement should be made at a height of between 1.2 m to 1.6 m above the deck, platform or walkway as follows:

   .1   at a distance of 1 m from, and at intervals not greater than 3 m around, all sources such as:

   –   main turbines or engines at each level

   –   main gearing

   –   turbo-blowers

   –   purifiers

   –   electrical alternators and generators

   –   boiler firing platform

   –   forced and/or induced draught fans

   –   compressors

   –   cargo pumps (including their driving motors or turbines)

   In order to avoid an unnecessarily large and impractical number of measurements and recordings in the case of large engines and of machinery spaces where the measured sound pressure level in dB(A) at the intervals above does not vary significantly, it will not be necessary to record each position. Full measurement at representative positions and at the positions of maximum sound pressure level shall, however, be made and recorded, subject to at least four measurements being recorded at each level;

   .2   at local control stations, e.g. the main manoeuvring or emergency manoeuvring stand on the main engine and the machinery control rooms;

   .3   at all other locations not specified in .1 and .2 which would normally be visited during routine inspection, adjustment and maintenance;

  .4 at points on all normally used access routes, unless covered by positions already specified above, at intervals not greater than 10 m; and

  .5 in rooms within the machinery space, e.g. workshops. In order to restrict the number of measurements and recordings, the number of recordings can be reduced as in .1, subject to a total of at least four measurements (including those specified in this paragraph) being recorded at each machinery space level up to upper deck.

3.12 Measurements in navigation spaces

Measurements shall be taken on both navigating bridge wings but should only be taken when the navigating bridge wing to be measured is on the lee side of the ship.

3.13 Measurements in accommodation spaces

3.13.1 One measurement shall be taken in the middle of the space. The microphone shall be moved slowly horizontally and/or vertically over a distance of 1 m (± 0.5 m, taking into account the measurement criteria in paragraph 3.10.1). Additional measurements should be performed at other points if appreciable differences, i.e. greater than 10 dB(A), in the level of sound inside the room occur, especially near the head positions of a sitting or lying person.

3.13.2 The number of measurement cabins shall be not less than 40% of total number of cabins. Cabins which are obviously affected by noise, i.e. cabins adjacent to machinery or casings, must be considered in any case.

3.13.3 For ships with a large number of crew cabins, such as passenger/ cruise ships, it will be acceptable to reduce the number of measurement positions. The selection of cabins to be tested shall be representative for the group of cabins being tested by selecting those cabins in closer proximity to noise sources, to the satisfaction of the Administration.

3.13.4 On open deck, measurements shall be taken in any areas provided for the purpose of recreation.

3.14   Measurements in normally unoccupied spaces

3.14.1   In addition to the spaces referred to in sections 3.10 to 3.13, measurements shall be taken in all locations with unusually high noise levels where seafarers may be exposed, even for relatively short periods, and at intermittently used machinery locations.

3.14.2   In order to restrict the number of measurements and recordings, noise levels need not be measured for normally unoccupied spaces, holds, deck areas and other spaces which are remote from sources of noise.

3.14.3   In cargo holds, at least three microphone positions in parts of holds where personnel are likely to carry out work shall be used.

Chapter 4
Maximum acceptable sound pressure levels

4.1   General

4.1.1   The limits specified in this section shall be regarded as maximum levels and not as desirable levels. Where reasonably practicable, it is desirable for the noise level to be lower than the maximum levels specified.

4.1.2   Before the ship is put in service, the limits specified in section 4.2 shall be assessed by the equivalent continuous sound level measurement for that space. In large rooms with many measurement positions the individual positions shall be compared to the limits.

4.1.3   Personnel entering spaces with nominal noise levels greater than 85 dB(A) should be required to wear hearing protectors while in those spaces (see chapter 5). The limit of 110 dB(A) given in paragraph 4.2.1 assumes that hearing protectors giving protection meeting the requirements for hearing protectors in chapter 7 are worn.

4.1.4   Limits are specified in terms of A-weighted sound pressure levels (see paragraphs 1.4.4 and 1.4.24).

4.2   Noise level limits

Limits for noise levels (dB(A)) are specified for various spaces as follows:

Designation of rooms and spaces	Ship size	
	1,600 up to 10,000 GT	≥ 10,000 GT
4.2.1 Work spaces (see 5.1)		
Machinery spaces[1]	110	110
Machinery control rooms	75	75
Workshops other than those forming part of machinery spaces	85	85
Non–specified workspaces (other work areas)[2]	85	85
4.2.2 Navigation spaces		
Navigating bridge and chartrooms	65	65
Look-out posts, incl. navigating bridge wings[3] and windows	70	70
Radio rooms (with radio equipment operating but not producing audio signals)	60	60
Radar rooms	65	65
4.2.3 Accommodation spaces		
Cabin and hospitals[4]	60	55
Messrooms	65	60
Recreation rooms	65	60
Open recreation areas (external recreation areas)	75	75
Offices	65	60
4.2.4 Service spaces		
Galleys, without food processing equipment operating	75	75
Serveries and pantries	75	75
4.2.5 Normally unoccupied spaces		
Spaces referred to in section 3.14	90	90

Notes

[1] If the maximum noise levels are exceeded when machinery is operating (only permitted if dispensation is granted in accordance with paragraph 1.3.6), exposure should be limited to very short periods or not allowed at all. The area should be marked according to section 7.4.

[2] Examples are open deck workspaces that are not machinery spaces, and open deck workspaces where communication is relevant.

[3] Reference is made to the Recommendation on methods of measuring noise levels at listening posts (resolution A.343(IX)) which also applies.

[4] Hospitals are treatment rooms with beds.

4.3 Survey report

4.3.1 A noise survey report shall be made for each ship. The report shall comprise information on the noise levels in the various spaces on board. The report shall show the reading at each specified measuring point. The points shall be marked on a general arrangement plan, or on accommodation drawings attached to the report, or shall otherwise be identified.

4.3.2 The format for noise survey reports is set out in appendix 1.

4.3.3 The noise survey report shall always be carried on board and be accessible for the crew.

Chapter 5
Noise exposure limits

5.1 General

5.1.1 The noise level limits as set out in chapter 4 are designed so that if they are complied with seafarers will not be exposed to an $L_{ex,24h}$ exceeding 80 dB(A), i.e. within each day or 24-hour period the equivalent continuous noise exposure would not exceed 80 dB(A). For a new ship, compliance with these criteria should be verified on the basis of sea trial measurements of noise levels by calculation of the expected noise exposure of each category of crew members in accordance with the method prescribed in section 3.7.

5.1.2 In spaces with sound pressure levels exceeding 85 dB(A), suitable hearing protection should be used, or to apply time limits for exposure, as set out in this section, to ensure that an equivalent level of protection is maintained.

5.1.3 Each ship to which these regulations apply should include in their Safety Management System a section on the company's policy regarding hearing protection, exposure limits and conduct training on those matters, which will be logged in their training records.

5.1.4 Consideration should be given to the instruction of seafarers on these aspects, as recorded in appendix 2. No crew member should be exposed unprotected to peak values exceeding 135 dB(C).

5.2 Conservation of hearing and use of hearing protectors

In order to comply with the exposure criteria of this section, the use of hearing protectors complying with chapter 7 is permitted. Even when hearing protectors are required for compliance with the Code, risk assessments, a hearing conservation programme and other measures may be implemented by the Administration.

5.3 Limits of exposure of seafarers to high noise levels

Seafarers should not be exposed to noise in excess of the levels and durations shown in figure 1 and described in paragraphs 5.3.1 to 5.3.5.

5.3.1 Maximum exposure with protection (zone A, figure 1)

No seafarer, even when wearing hearing protectors, should be exposed to levels exceeding 120 dB(A) or to an $L_{eq,24h}$ exceeding 105 dB(A).

5.3.2 Occasional exposure (zone B, figure 1)

Only occasional exposures should be allowed in zone B and hearing protectors with an attenuation between 25 and 35 dB(A) should be used.

5.3.3 Occasional exposure (zone C, figure 1)

In zone C, only occasional exposures should be allowed and hearing protectors with an attenuation of at least 25 dB(A) should be used.

5.3.4 Daily exposure (zone D, figure 1)

If seafarers routinely work (daily exposure) in spaces with noise levels within zone D hearing protectors with an attenuation up to at least 25 dB(A) should be used and risk assessment and a hearing conservation programme may be considered.

5.3.5 Maximum exposure without protection (zone E, figure 1)

For exposures of less than eight hours, seafarers without hearing protection should not be exposed to noise levels exceeding 85 dB(A). When seafarers remain for more than eight hours in spaces with a high noise level, an $L_{eq,24h}$ of 80 dB(A) should not be exceeded. Consequently, for at least a third of each 24 h each seafarer should be subject to an environment with a noise level below 75 dB(A).

5.4 24-hour equivalent continuous sound level limit

As an alternative to compliance with the provisions of section 5.3 (figure 1), no unprotected seafarer should be exposed to a 24-hour equivalent continuous sound level greater than 80 dB(A). Each individual's daily exposure duration in spaces requiring the use of hearing protectors should not exceed four hours continuously or eight hours in total.

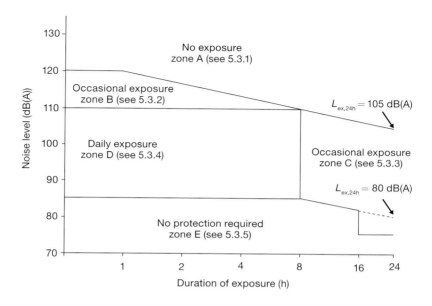

Figure 1 – *Allowable daily and occasionally occupational zones*

Note: To work in zones A to D, hearing protectors attenuating the sound to the ear down to below 85 dB(A) are required. To work in zone E, hearing protectors are not required but should be accessible if the sound level is over 80 dB(A) for more than eight hours.

5.5   Hearing conservation programme

5.5.1   A hearing conservation programme may be provided for seafarers working in spaces with $L_{Aeq} > 85$ dB(A) in order to train them in the hazards of noise and use of hearing protection, and to monitor hearing acuity. Some elements of a hearing conservation programme are as follows:

.1   Initial and periodic audiometric tests administered by a trained and appropriately qualified person, to the satisfaction of the Administration.

.2   Instruction of exposed persons on the hazards of high and long duration noise exposures and on the proper use of ear protectors (see appendix 2).

> **.3**   Maintenance of audiometric test records.
>
> **.4**   Periodic analysis of records and hearing acuity of individuals with high-hearing loss.

5.5.2   An optional element of a hearing conservation programme is to control the 24-hour equivalent continuous sound level to which individuals working in high noise level spaces are exposed. Such control requires calculation of the 24-hour equivalent continuous sound level. If this 24-hour level does not meet the limits, the duration of exposure should be controlled or hearing protectors used at appropriate times to bring the individual's exposure within the limit.

Chapter 6
Acoustic insulation between accommodation spaces

6.1   General

Consideration shall be given to the acoustic insulation between accommodation spaces in order to make rest and recreation possible even if activities are going on in adjacent spaces, e.g. music, talking, cargo handling, etc.

6.2   Sound insulation index

6.2.1   The airborne sound insulation properties for bulkheads and decks within the accommodation shall comply at least with the following weighted sound reduction index (R_w) according to ISO Standard 717-1:1996, as amended (1:2013), part 1:[*]

Cabin to cabin	$R_w = 35$
Meal rooms, recreation rooms, public spaces and entertainment areas for cabins and hospitals	$R_w = 45$
Corridor to cabin	$R_w = 30$
Cabin to cabin with communicating door	$R_w = 30$

6.2.2   The airborne sound insulation properties shall be determined by laboratory tests in accordance with ISO 10140-2:2010, to the satisfaction of the Administration.

---

[*]   ISO Standard 717-1 – Acoustics – Rating of sound insulation in buildings and of building elements – part 1: Airborne sound insulation, and its amendment published in 2013.

6.3 Erection of materials

6.3.1 Care should be taken in the erection of materials and in the construction of accommodation spaces. During sea trial testing, if the erection of materials is in doubt then measurements should be taken on board ships for a representative selection of each type of partition, floors, doors, etc. as requested in paragraph 6.2.1 and to the satisfaction of the Administration.

6.3.2 The apparent weighted sound reduction index R'_w should comply with the requirements of the paragraph 6.2.1 with tolerance of up to 3 dB.

Note: Field measurements should be performed according to ISO 140-4:1998.[*] When the area of the materials tested is < 10 m², a minimum value of 10 m² should be considered for the calculation of the R'_w index.

---

[*] ISO 140-4 Acoustics – Measurement of sound insulation in buildings and of building elements – part 4: field measurements of airborne sound insulation between rooms.

Chapter 7
Hearing protection and warning information

7.1   General

When the application of means for controlling sound at source does not reduce the noise level in any space to that specified in paragraph 4.1.3, seafarers who are required to enter such spaces shall be supplied with effective hearing protection on an individual basis. The provision of hearing protectors shall not be considered to be a substitute for effective noise control. Appendix 3 summarizes current noise abatement methods which may be applied on new ships.

7.2   Requirements for hearing protectors

7.2.1   The individual hearing protectors shall be so selected as to eliminate the risk to hearing or to reduce the risk to an acceptable level as specified in paragraph 7.2.2. The ship operator shall make every effort to ensure the wearing of hearing protectors and shall be responsible for checking the effectiveness of measures taken in compliance with this Code.

7.2.2   Hearing protectors shall be of a type such that they can reduce sound pressure levels to 85 dB(A) or less (see section 5.1). Selection of suitable hearing protectors should be in accordance with the HML-method described in ISO 4869-2:1994 (see explanation and example in appendix 2). Noise-cancelling technology may be used if the headsets have equivalent performance to hearing protectors in their unpowered condition.

7.2.2.1   Noise-cancelling headsets specifications should be as per confirmed manufacturer specifications.

7.3   Selection and use of hearing protectors

Seafarers should be instructed in the proper use of hearing protectors as provided or used on board in accordance with appendix 2.

7.4   Warning notices

Where the noise level in machinery spaces (or other spaces) is greater than 85 dB(A), entrances to such spaces shall carry a warning notice comprising symbol and supplementary sign in the working language of the ship as prescribed by the Administration (see below an example of the warning notice and signs in English). If only a minor portion of the space has such noise levels the particular location(s) or equipment shall be identified at eye level, visible from each direction of access.

Signs at the entrance to noisy rooms (example in English)

80 dB(A) to 85 dB(A)	HIGH-NOISE LEVEL – USE HEARING PROTECTORS
85 dB(A) to 110 dB(A)	DANGEROUS NOISE – USE OF HEARING PROTECTORS MANDATORY
110 dB(A) to 115 dB(A)	CAUTION: DANGEROUS NOISE – USE OF HEARING PROTECTORS MANDATORY – SHORT STAY ONLY
> 115 dB(A)	CAUTION: EXCESSIVELY HIGH-NOISE LEVEL – USE OF HEARING PROTECTORS MANDATORY – NO STAY LONGER THAN 10 MINUTES

Appendix 1
Format for noise survey report

1   Ship particulars

.1   Name of ship

.2   Port of registry

.3   Name and address of shipowner, managing owner or agent

.4   Name and address of shipbuilder

.5   Place of build

.6   IMO number

.7   Gross tonnage

.8   Type of ship

.9   Ship's dimensions

- length
- breadth
- depth
- maximum draught (summer load line)

.10   Displacement at maximum draught

.11   Date of keel laying

.12   Date of delivery

2   Machinery particulars

.1   Propulsion machinery

- manufacturer
- type
- number of units

		maximum continuous rating – power	kW
		normal designed service shaft speed	rpm
		normal service rating – power	kW

.2 Auxiliary diesel engines
- manufacturer
- type
- number of units
- output   kW

.3 Main reduction gear

.4 Propellers
- type of propeller (fixed, controllable pitch, Voith-Schneider)
- number of propellers
- number of blades
- designed propeller shaft speed   rpm

.5 Other (in case of special propulsion and power configurations)

.6 Engine room ventilation
- manufacturer
- type
- number of units
- fan diameter   m
- fan speed   rpm
- variable speed (Y/N)
- airflow capacity m^3/h
- total pressure   Pa

3   Measuring instrumentation and personnel

.1 Instrumentation   Make   Type   Serial no.
- sound level meter
- microphone
- filter
- windscreen

– calibrator
– other equipment

.2 Calibration of sound level meter at survey
by competent authority

– date
– calibration
– start
– finish

.3 Identification of persons/organizations carrying out
measurements

4 Conditions during measurement

.1 Date of measurement

– starting time
– completion time

.2 Ship's position during measurement

.3 Loading condition of the ship

.4 Conditions during measurement

– draught forward
– draught aft
– depth of water under keel

.5 Weather conditions

– wind force
– sea state

.6 Ship speed

.7 Actual propeller shaft speed   rpm

.8 Propeller pitch

.9 Propulsion machinery speed   rpm

.10 Propulsion machinery power   kW

.11 Number of propulsion machinery units operating

.12 Number of diesel auxiliary engines operating

.13   Number of turbogenerators operating

.14   Engine room ventilation speed mode (high/low/variable)

.15   Engine load (% MCR)

.16   Other auxiliary equipment operating

     –   ventilation, heating and air conditioning equipment in operation

5   Measuring data

Noise limits dB(A)	Measured sound pressure levels	
	L_{Aeq}	dB(A)
	L_{Ceq}	dB(C)
	L_{Cpeak}	dB(C)

Note: Measurement of sound pressure level L_{Ceq} and L_{Cpeak} should be done only in the case of noise levels exceeding 85 dB(A) and hearing protectors are required.

Work spaces

–   machinery spaces

–   machinery control rooms

–   workshops

–   non-specified workspaces

Navigation spaces

–   navigating bridge and chartrooms

–   look-out posts, including navigating bridge wings and windows

–   radio rooms

–   radar rooms

Accommodation spaces

–   cabins and hospitals

–   meal rooms

–   recreation rooms

–   open recreation areas

–   offices

Service spaces

–   galleys, without food processing equipment operating

–   serveries and pantries

Normally unoccupied spaces

6   Main noise abatement measures
(list measures taken)

7   Remarks
(list any exceptions to the Code)

....

....

....

Name   ....

Address   ....

                     ....

....

                Place   Date   Signature

Attachment: Pages of frequency analysis

Frequency analysis for certain areas may result in more accurate and precise noise level predictions and will aid in the detection of specific frequency bands which exceed the established limits in chapter 4. Further guidance may be found in ISO 1996-2:2007.

Appendix 2
Guidance on the inclusion of noise issues in safety management systems

1   Instruction to seafarers

1.1   Seafarers should be instructed in the hazards of high and long duration noise exposures and the risk of noise-induced hearing loss. Instruction should be given to all seafarers on initial employment and periodically thereafter to those regularly working in spaces with noise levels in excess of 85 dB(A). Instruction in the provisions of the Code should include:

> .1   noise exposure limits and the use of warning notices;

> .2   the types of hearing protectors provided, their approximate attenuation and their proper use, fitting, and the effects on normal communications when first wearing such protection;

> .3   company policies and procedures related to hearing protection and where appropriate any monitoring programme which may be available for seafarers working in spaces covered by warning notices; and

> .4   guidance on the possible signs of hearing loss such as ringing in the ear, dead ear, or fullness in the ear and mitigating techniques to be effected when those signs occur.

1.2   Appropriate seafarers should receive such instruction as is necessary in the correct use and maintenance of machinery and silencers or attenuators in order to avoid the production of unnecessary noise.

2   Responsibility of ship operators

2.1   The ship operator should be responsible for ensuring that means for noise reduction and control are applied and maintained such that the requirements of the Code are met.

2.2   Where noise levels in any space exceed the limit of 85 dB(A), shipowners should ensure that:

.1   the space is identified and relevant provisions of the Code are complied with;

.2   the master and senior officers of the ship are aware of the importance of controlling entry into the space and the importance of the use of suitable hearing protection;

.3   suitable and sufficient hearing protection is provided for distribution on an individual basis to all relevant crew members; and

.4   the master, senior officers and any safety officer on board a ship are aware of the need for the relevant training and information to be provided on board.

2.3   Where hand tools, galley and other portable equipment produce noise levels above 85 dB(A) in normal working conditions, shipowners should ensure that warning information should be provided.

3   Responsibility of seafarers

Seafarers should be made aware of the need to ensure that:

.1   all measures adopted for noise control are utilized;

.2   any defective noise control equipment is reported to responsible persons under the ship's safety management system;

.3   suitable hearing protectors are always worn when entering areas in which their use is required by warning notices and that those protectors are not removed in those spaces, even for short periods; and

.4   the hearing protectors provided for their use are not damaged or misused and are maintained in a sanitary condition.

4   Selection of hearing protectors

4.1   Selection of suitable hearing protectors should be carried out according to the HML-method described in ISO 4869-2:1994. In order to give guidance to ship operators and seafarers in choosing proper hearing protection, a short description of the HML-method and its use is given in 4.2.

4.2 The HML-method is a rating which is calculated in accordance with ISO 4869-2:1994, Estimation of effective A-weighted sound pressure levels when hearing protectors are worn. Using the H, M, and L ratings requires both A-weighted (L_{Aeq}) and C-weighted (L_{Ceq}) sound pressure levels of the noise and the HML values for the hearing protector in question, which will be provided by the manufacturer.

4.2.1 The HML values for a hearing protector are related to the attenuation that the protector offers in noise of high, medium and low frequencies. These H and M values are used in the calculation of the protected exposure level for noises which have primary energy in the middle and high frequencies. This is considered the case if the measured L_{Ceq} and L_{Aeq} levels differ by 2 dB or less.

4.2.2 The M and L values for the hearing protector are used in the calculation of the protected exposure level for noises which have appreciable low-frequency components and for which the measured L_{Ceq} and L_{Aeq} levels differ by more than 2 dB in those spaces where the protector is intended to be used.

4.3 An example of simple use of the HML method

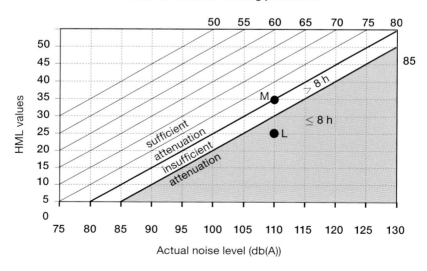

Noise level inside hearing protectors

On a given ship, the measured sound level in the machinery room is 110 dB(A), 115 dB(C). The chosen hearing protectors have the following attenuation according to the manufacturer: H = 35 dB, M = 30 dB and L = 20 dB.

.1 Mark the hearing protectors' L and M values on the vertical line starting at the actual noise level (110 dB(A)).

.2 Settle if the noise has low or high/medium frequency. If $L_{Ceq} - L_{Aeq}$ is more than 2 dB, the noise has low frequency (L) and if $L_{Ceq} - L_{Aeq}$ is less than 2 dB, the noise has high or medium frequency (M).

.3 If the sound is of high/medium frequency ($L_{Ceq} - L_{Aeq} \leq 2$ dB), follow the diagonal line from the M-value and take a reading of the noise level inside the hearing protectors. In this case, the noise level inside the hearing protectors is 80 dB(A) which means that the attenuation of the hearing protectors are sufficient for work over eight hours a day.

.4 If the sound has low frequency ($L_{Ceq} - L_{Aeq} > 2$ dB), follow the diagonal lines from the L-value and take a reading of the noise level inside the hearing protectors. In this case, the noise level inside the hearing protectors is greater than 85 dB(A) which means that the hearing protectors are not good enough for a working day of eight hours. Choose a hearing protector that has an L-value above 25 dB instead.

4.4 Calculation by the HML-method – principle and example

Determination of feasibility of a particular protector in a specific noise environment can also be calculated. The values H, M and L may be used to estimate L'_A (total A-weighted noise level at the ear) for a particular protector in specific noise situation.

.1 Calculate $L_{Ceq} - L_{Aeq}$ (This requires measurements of L_{Aeq} and L_{Ceq}. All class 1 sound level meters can apply A-weighted or C-weighted.)

.2 If $L_{Ceq} - L_{Aeq} \leq 2$ dB, the predicted noise reduction level (PNR) is calculated using the equation:

$$PNR = M - \left(\frac{H - M}{4}\right)\left(L_{Ceq} - L_{Aeq} - 2\right)$$

If $L_{Ceq} - L_{Aeq} > 2$ dB, PNR is calculated using the equation:

$$PNR = M - \left(\frac{M - L}{8}\right)\left(L_{Ceq} - L_{Aeq} - 2\right)$$

.3   The PNR is then subtracted from the total A-weighted noise level to give the effective A-weighted level at the ear under the protector L'_A:

$$L'_A = L_{Aeq} - PNR$$

Example

Hearing protector: H = 35 dB, M = 25 dB, L = 20 dB

Noise level in engine-room:

$L_{Aeq} = 108.7$ dB(A)

$L_{Ceq} = 109.0$ dB(C)

$L_{Ceq} - L_{Aeq} = 0.3$ dB

$PNR = 25 - (\frac{35 - 25}{4})(0.3 - 2) = 29.3$ dB

$L'_A = 108.7 - 29.3 = 79.4$ dB(A)

In this case, the noise level inside the hearing protectors is below 80 dB(A) which means that the attenuation of the hearing protectors is sufficient for work over eight hours a day.

Appendix 3
Suggested methods of attenuating noise

1   General

1.1   In order to obtain a noise reduction on board ships to comply with the limits given in chapters 4 and 5 of the Code, careful consideration should be given to means of such reduction. This appendix is intended to provide information for the design of a ship in this respect.

1.2   Design and construction of noise control measures should be supervised by persons skilled in noise control techniques.

1.3   Some of the measures which can be taken to control the noise level or reduce the exposure of seafarers to potentially harmful noise are indicated in sections 2 to 10 of this appendix. It is emphasized that it will not be necessary to implement all or any of the measures recommended in this appendix on all ships. This Code does not provide detailed technical information needed for putting constructional noise control measures into effect, or for deciding which measures are appropriate in particular circumstances.

1.4   In applying noise control measures, care should be taken to ensure that rules and regulations concerning ship structure, accommodation and other safety matters are not infringed and the use of sound reduction materials should not introduce fire, safety or health hazards nor should such material, by virtue of flimsy construction or attachment, introduce hazards that may tend to impede either evacuation or dewatering of the spaces.

1.5   The need for noise control should be taken into account at the design stage when deciding which of different designs of engines and machinery are to be installed, the method of installation and the siting of machinery in relation to other spaces, and the acoustic insulation and siting of the accommodation spaces.

1.6   Due to the normal method of ship construction, it is most probable that noise originating from machinery and propellers reaching the accommodation and other spaces outside the machinery spaces will be of the structure-borne type.

1.7   When designing efficient and economic measures for noise control of machinery installations in existing ships, the measurement of sound produced in terms of A-weighted sound level may need to be supplemented by some form of frequency analysis.

2   Isolation of sources of noise

2.1   Where practicable, any engines or machinery producing noise levels in excess of the limits set out in section 4.2 of the Code should be installed in compartments which do not require continuous attendance (see also paragraph 6.1 of this appendix).

2.2   Accommodation should be sited both horizontally and vertically as far away as is practicable from sources of noise such as propellers and propulsion machinery.

2.3   Machinery casings should, where practicable, be arranged outside superstructures and deckhouses containing accommodation spaces. Where this is not feasible, passageways should be arranged between the casings and accommodation spaces, if practicable.

2.4   Consideration should be given, where practicable, to the placing of accommodation spaces in deck houses not in superstructures extending to the ship's side.

2.5   Consideration may also be given, where applicable, to the separation of accommodation spaces from machinery spaces by unoccupied spaces, sanitary and washing rooms.

2.6   Suitable partitions, bulkheads, decks, etc. may be needed to prevent the spread of sound. It is important that these be of the correct construction and location in relation to the source of sound and the frequency of the sound to be attenuated.

2.7   Where a space, such as a machinery space, is being divided into noisy (not continually manned) and less noisy (capable of being continually manned) spaces, it is preferable to have complete separation.[*]

2.8   It may be advisable to provide sound absorbing material in certain spaces in order to prevent increase of noise level due to reflection from partitions, bulkheads, decks, etc.

---

[*] In these cases, it may be necessary to ensure the supervision of the plant by installing alarms in the less noisy compartments and to arrange means of escape so that seafarers may leave these compartments without danger.

3   Exhaust and intake silencing

3.1   Exhaust systems from internal combustion engines, air-intake systems to machinery spaces, accommodation spaces and other spaces should be so arranged that the inflow or discharge orifices are remote from places frequented by seafarers.

3.2   Silencers, noise-cancelling equipment or attenuators should be fitted when necessary.

3.3   To minimize accommodation noise levels it is normally necessary to reduce structure-borne noise by isolating exhaust systems and certain pipe work and duct work from casings, bulkheads, etc.

4   Machinery enclosure

4.1   In continuously manned spaces or spaces where seafarers might reasonably be expected to spend lengthy periods of time on maintenance or overhaul work, and where separation as detailed in section 2 of this appendix is not practicable, consideration should be given to the fitting of sound insulating enclosures or partial enclosures to engines or machinery producing sound pressure levels in excess of the limits set out in section 4.2 of the Code.

4.2   Where the noise level produced by engines or machinery installed in spaces as in paragraph 4.1 above falls within the criteria of paragraph 5.3.1 of the Code and zone A of figure 1, it is essential that noise reduction measures are provided.

4.3   When sound insulating enclosures are fitted, it is important that they entirely enclose the noise source.

5   Reduction of noise in the aft body

To reduce the noise influence in the aft body of the ship, especially to the accommodation spaces, consideration may be given to noise emission problems during the design procedures relating to the aft body, propeller, etc.

6   Enclosure of the operator

6.1   In most machinery spaces it would be desirable and advisable to protect operating or watchkeeping seafarers by providing a sound-reducing control room or other similar space (see paragraph 2.1 of this appendix).

6.2   In continuously manned machinery spaces of small ships and of existing ships where noise levels are in excess of 85 dB(A), it would be desirable to provide a noise refuge at the control station or manoeuvring platform where the watch keeper might be expected to spend the major part of the time.

7   Control of noise accentuation into accommodation spaces

7.1   To reduce noise levels in accommodation spaces it may be necessary to consider the isolation of deckhouses containing such spaces from the remaining structure of the ship by resilient mountings.

7.2   Consideration may also be given to the provision of flexible connections to bulkheads, linings and ceilings and the installation of floating floors within accommodation spaces.

7.3   The provision of curtains to side scuttles and windows and the use of carpets within accommodation spaces assist in absorbing noise.

8   Selection of machinery

8.1   The sound produced by each item of machinery to be fitted should be taken into account at the design stage. It may be possible to control noise by using a machine producing less airborne, fluid-borne or structure-borne sound.

8.2   Manufacturers should be requested to supply information on the sound produced by their machinery and also to provide recommended methods of installation in order to keep noise levels to a minimum.

9   Inspection and maintenance

All items of machinery, equipment and associated working spaces should be periodically inspected as part of the onboard safety management system with respect to any noise control/reduction features. Should such inspection reveal defects in the means for noise control, or other defects causing excessive noise, these should be rectified as soon as is practical.

10   Vibration isolation

10.1   Where necessary, machines should be supported on carefully selected resilient mountings. To ensure the effectiveness of the isolation, the mountings should be installed on a sufficient stiff foundation.

10.2 Where structure-borne sound from auxiliary machinery, compressors, hydraulic units, generating sets, vents, exhaust pipes and silencers produces unacceptable noise levels in accommodation spaces or on the navigating bridge, use of resilient mountings should be considered.

10.3 When sound insulating enclosures are fitted consideration may be given to the machine being resiliently mounted and pipe, trunk and cable connections to it being flexible.

11 Noise prediction

11.1 In the design phase of new ships, the designer/yard may predict by calculations, qualified assessments or the like, the expected noise levels in areas of the ship likely to have noise levels over acceptable levels from chapter 4.

11.2 The noise predictions referred to in paragraph 11.1 should be used in the design phase to identify possible areas in the ship where special consideration must be given to noise reduction measures in order to observe the noise level limits stipulated in section 4.2 of the Code.

11.3 The noise predictions and any noise reduction measures planned in the design phase should be documented, especially in cases where, according to the noise predictions, it must be expected that compliance with any of the noise level limits of section 4.2 of the Code will be difficult to achieve, despite reasonable technical initiatives.

12 Noise-cancelling equipment

12.1 Noise cancellation, also known as anti-noise, is the process whereby mostly low-frequency (below 500 Hz) repetitive noises such as made by engines and rotating machinery, is cancelled out by introducing a cancelling anti-noise signal which is equal to but 180 degrees out of phase with the noise. This anti-noise is introduced to the environment in a way that it matches the noise in the region of interest. The two signals then cancel each other out, effectively removing a significant portion of the noise energy from the environment.

12.2 Several applications for this technology exist. They include:

.1 Active mufflers: these have been shown in other modes of transportation to reduce exhaust noise from internal combustion engines, compressors, and vacuum pumps without the inefficiencies caused by back pressure.

.2   Active mounts: these can contain vibration from rotating machines to improve comfort, decrease wear on moving parts, and reduce secondary acoustic noise from vibration.

.3   Noise-cancelled quiet zones: currently silent seats and (automobile) cabin quieting systems for various modes of transportation exist. The possibility exists for producing active-quieted bunks of other spaces for seafarer comfort and recovery.

.4   Noise-cancelling headsets: these can extend hearing protection beyond passive ear defenders to include low frequencies. Active headsets can also allow communication, by permitting normal conversation, and improve workplace safety.

12.3   It is suggested that information concerning experience from these active noise-reducing systems be provided to the Organization to better evaluate the performance parameters of these systems.

13   Noise recovery areas

13.1   Incorporation of noise recovery areas may be used as an alternative design approach for the construction of ships under 1,600 GT or ice-breaking vessels. Noise recovery areas may also be considered for incorporation in ship-specific applications where noisy operations (examples are extended air/helicopter operations or heavy weather operation of dynamic positioning equipment) are undertaken for time periods over and above those of normal, routine seagoing practices. The use of these spaces should be integrated into ship safe operations policies under the ISM Code.

13.2   Noise recovery areas should be provided if no other technical or organizational solutions are feasible to reduce excessive noise from sound sources.

Appendix 4
Simplified procedure for determining noise exposure

1   General

1.1   In order to ensure that seafarers will not be exposed to an $L_{ex,24h}$ exceeding 80 dB(A), this appendix is providing information on a simplified procedure for determining the related noise exposure.

1.2   The determination of noise exposure should be usually carried out based on ISO 9612:2009.

1.3   A simplified method based on the noise measurements during sea trail/harbour stay and a job profile for crew members is described in the following.

2   Work analysis/job profiling and off-duty hours

2.1   With the help of a crew list, different job categories (groups) will be defined.

For example:

–   master

–   chief engineer

–   electrician

–   cook

–   etc.

2.2   For each job category, a job profile has to be defined individually. The job profile is related to the work spaces on board the vessel.

For example:

–   wheelhouse

–   ship office

     –   machinery control room

     –   workshop

     –   engine-room

     –   galley

     –   etc.

2.3   For each job category, the working shift is to be divided into partitions (i) related to the work spaces. A similar assessment should be made for off-duty hours (the partitions are based on estimations by the owner/operator/employer).

Example

A full day for an electrician may be divided into the following partitions:

$i = 1$	Workshop	=	$T_i = 5$ h
$i = 2$	Machinery control room	=	$T_i = 2$ h
$i = 3$	Ship office	=	$T_i = 2$ h
$i = 4$	Engine-room	=	$T_i = 1$ h
$i = 5$	Off duty	=	$T_i = 14$ h
	Total	=	$T_{total} = 24$ h

3   Determination of estimated noise exposure levels

3.1   Based on the noise report and the estimated working times and off-duty hours for each job category, the noise exposure level can be calculated. It is assumed that the noise limits for cabins and recreation spaces according to this Code will not be exceeded. Using well-selected hearing protectors is recommendatory according to this Code. It is assumed that the maximum noise level of workers wearing hearing protectors does not exceed 85 dB(A).

3.2 The noise contribution from each space is calculated as follows:

$$L_{ex,24h,i} = L_{Aeq,i} + 10\log\left(\frac{T_i}{T_0}\right)$$

where:

T_i is the effective duration on board for each space

T_0 is the reference duration 24 h

$L_{Aeq,i}$ is the A-weighted equivalent continuous sound level for each space

3.3 The A-weighted noise exposure level is calculated from the noise contribution from each space as follows:

$$L_{ex,24h} = 10\log\left(\sum_{i=1}^{n} 10\frac{L_{ex,24h,i}}{10}\right)$$

Example

Result sheet

Job category	**Electrician**	Location/space						
		Navigating bridge	Ship office	Machinery control room	Workshops	Engine-room	Galley	Off duty
Measured A-weighted equivalent continuous sound level $L_{Aeq,i}$ (dB(A))		64	63	75	84	85	72	60
Duration/ stay T_i (h)		0	2	2	5	1	0	14
Noise contribution $L_{ex,24h,i}$ (dB)		0	52.2	64.2	77.2	71.2	0	57.7
A-weighted noise exposure level $L_{ex,24h}$ (dB)	**78.3**							

Notes

Notes